The Library of Author Biographies™

Madeleine L'Engle

Madeleine L'Engle

The Library of Author Biographies™

MADELEINE L'ENGLE

Aaron Rosenberg

rosen central™

The Rosen Publishing Group, Inc., New York

Published in 2006 by The Rosen Publishing Group, Inc.
29 East 21st Street, New York, NY 10010

First Edition

Library of Congress Cataloging-in-Publication Data

Rosenberg, Aaron.
Madeleine L'Engle/Aaron Rosenberg.—1st ed.
    p. cm.—(The library of author biographies)
Includes bibliographical references and index.
ISBN 1-4042-0466-0 (lib. bdg.)
ISBN 1-4042-0650-7 (pbk. bdg.)
1. L'Engle, Madeleine. 2. Authors, American—20th century—Biography.
I. Title. II. Series.
PS3523.E55Z87 2006
813'.54—dc22

                                                    2004027660

Manufactured in the United States of America

Reprinted by permission of Farrar, Straus and Giroux, LLC. Excerpts from A WRINKLE IN TIME by Madeleine L'Engle. Copyright © 1962, renewed 1990 by Madeleine L'Engle Franklin.
Reprinted by permission of Farrar, Straus and Giroux, LLC. Excerpts from THE SUMMER OF THE GREAT-GRANDMOTHER by Madeleine L'Engle. Copyright © 1974 by Crosswicks Ltd.
Excerpts from THE CIRCLE OF QUIET by Madeleine L'Engle. Copyright © 1972 by Madeleine L'Engle Franklin. Reprinted by permission of Farrar, Straus and Giroux, LLC.
Courtesy of Amazon.com. All rights reserved.
Reprinted by permission of Farrar, Straus and Giroux, LLC. Excerpts from TWO-PART INVENTION by Madeleine L'Engle. Copyright © 1988 by Crosswicks Ltd.
Reprinted from Penguins and Golden Calves. Copyright © 1996, 2003 by Crosswicks, Inc. WaterBrook Press, Colorado Springs, CO. All rights reserved.
From Newsweek, May 7, 2004 © 2004 Newsweek, Inc. All rights reserved. Reprinted by permission.
Quotations excerpted from the Writer Hero: Madeleine L'Engle story written by Karen Pritzker for The MY HERO Project (http://myheroproject.org).
Scaperlanda, María Ruiz. "Madeleine L'Engle: An Epic in Time." St. Anthony Messenger, June 2000.
Excerpt from "Author Spotlight: Madeleine L'Engle," Random House Online. (http://www.randomhouse.com/kids/author/results_spotlight.pperl?author id=16446) Used by permission of Random House, Inc.

Table of Contents

Introduction:
A Teller of Stories

The world is filled with authors. Ever since people first told stories around the tribal fire, some people have devoted their lives to telling stories. And once people started printing and selling their stories, some of those storytellers decided to become authors. Today, many people have stories to tell, and many of those people are convinced they can make a living selling their stories. Some of these people fail. Others succeed. But only a handful have long careers, and only a few of those make a lasting impression on their readers.

Madeleine L'Engle is one of those few. Over her sixty-year career she has written more than sixty books, and won an impressive array of awards. But that is not what makes her so impressive. It is her skill with words, stories, and truths that has made her one of the greatest children's book authors of our time.

Furthermore, L'Engle does not limit herself to one type of writing. She has written books for children, plays, poems, essays, and novels for adults. Her work has ranged from science fiction and fantasy to autobiography to mystery to religious essay. But in every case, she has explored the same themes, and espoused the same views.

Perhaps what makes L'Engle such a great writer, and has won her such affection from her readers, is her tone. She never talks down to her readers, whether they are children or adults, nor does she differentiate between them. For L'Engle, the story is the key. The audience comes later. She has told interviewers before that she has never set out to write a children's book versus an adult book—she simply writes, and then finds a home for the story when it is finished.

This may be why some critics claim L'Engle's work is not suited for children. They accuse her of writing stories that are too dark and depressing. It is true that most of her novels deal with death in some form. *Meet the Austins* (1960), for example, starts with the Austin family coping with the death of a beloved uncle. But death is a fact of life. She does not believe children should be shielded from such dark truths—instead, she wants them to face death and other sorrows, so the children can learn to deal with these issues early in life, and not be overwhelmed by them later. L'Engle also believes that children are more open-minded than adults, and can grasp new concepts more easily. "If I have something that is too difficult for adults to swallow, then I will write it in a book for children."[1]

Another reason some critics disapprove of L'Engle is her religion. She is unabashedly Christian, and most of her books have Christian elements or overtones. This offends some people. At the same time, many conservative Christians dislike her because she refuses to conform to church beliefs. L'Engle admits she is heavily religious. For her, writing is a form of prayer. But she also admits that she is always looking for answers. She sees nothing wrong with being angry with God when bad things happen. For her, faith is an intellectual process, and religion is all about asking questions and seeking answers. Her books often contain obvious good and evil characters, such as Charles Wallace's good, mysterious friend Mrs. Whatsit and the evil, disembodied brain IT in *A Wrinkle in Time* (1962). They also contain questionable characters, like the deceptive Kali Cutter in *The Arm of the Starfish* (1965). L'Engle's characters never lecture readers about religion, or expect everyone to believe the same thing they do. Neither does L'Engle, who considers anyone with faith and the desire to learn to be her religious equal.

Then there is her refusal to be pigeonholed. She has written for a variety of genres, often in the same book—one novel might deal with religion, myth, and science all at once, while another straddles the gap between fantasy, science fiction, and mystery. She writes the stories that come to her and does not worry about how people will classify them until later.

Even L'Engle's critics like her characters. Most of the people in her books are extremely likable and very believable. She has a gift for describing characters in just a few words, capturing not only their looks, but also their personality, as she does when we first meet Calvin O'Keefe in *A Wrinkle in Time*:

> Just because I'm tall. Calvin sounded a little embarrassed. Tall he certainly was, and skinny. His boney wrists stuck out of the sleeves of his blue sweater; his worn corduroy trousers were three inches too short. He had orange hair that needed cutting, and the appropriate freckles to go with it. His eyes were oddly bright blue.[2]

In part, L'Engle's characters are so vivid because she bases them on herself and those close to her. But it is also her power of imagination that brings them to life. Her characters are usually bright, pleasant people who have trouble being understood, and who feel out of place. These are characters the readers can identify with, particularly children and teenagers, and also people they would like to see succeed. And, in most of her books, L'Engle's characters do succeed. Her novels are not always uplifting. They do not always have happy endings—a major character dies toward the end of *The Arm of the Starfish*—but they have believable endings. Most of her characters make a real effort to learn and grow, and are rewarded for the pain they've suffered.

L'Engle believes that pain is a necessary part of life. Her characters feel a full range of emotions and experience sorrow and grief as well as joy and contentment. Without those darker emotions, they would not be able to appreciate the happier ones later. Characters who only have good things happen to them are not believable, not real. The readers cannot learn anything from them.

L'Engle's books teach a great deal. Every work is filled with the same themes and focuses on what she considers important in life. Family is first, and friendship a close second. Taking responsibility for your own actions and determining your own course in life are also important. Her characters often battle evil, but the evils are neglect, anger, and self-doubt, and are rarely fought with violence. In *A Wrinkle in Time*, for example, Meg combats evil with love. L'Engle does not approve of violence, but she does encourage people to stand up for themselves and to appreciate the good things in their lives. Judging from the number of people who still consider her their favorite author, she herself is one of those good things.

1 Early Madeleine

Madeleine L'Engle was born Madeleine L'Engle Camp in New York City on November 29, 1918. She was named after her great-grandmother, whose proper name was Madeleine L'Engle but whom the family generally referred to as Mado. As L'Engle remembers, "Mado died a year before I was born, and yet I feel that I have always known her, the stories about her are so vivid."[1]

L'Engle's mother, Madeleine Hall Barnett Camp, was a gifted pianist from Jacksonville, Florida. Her father, Charles Wadsworth Camp, who was from New Jersey, graduated from Princeton University and was a writer and journalist. The Camps had wanted a child for many years but had been unable to have one.

Madeleine Camp was almost forty when she finally got pregnant, and had, in fact, been advised to abort her pregnancy because her doctor had the opinion that both she and the baby would not survive. But she was determined to have a child, and found another doctor, a Catholic this time, who did not believe in abortion and who assured her that they would somehow manage to save both mother and baby. Young Madeleine was the result.

Despite her parents' strong desire to have her, Madeleine was often left to her own devices or in the care of her English nanny, Mrs. O'Connell. The Camps were busy, creative, and social people, and their lives were already full before Madeleine was born. They did not want to give up their friends and social activities just to care for her. As a result, young Madeleine often found herself alone in their Manhattan apartment, and turned to reading for solace and escape. Her favorite author was Lucy Maud Montgomery, who is best known for her *Anne of Green Gables* books. But Madeleine preferred Montgomery's book *Emily of New Moon* because she had more in common with its heroine. She explains:

> Emily was an only child, as I was. Emily lived on an island, as did I. Although Manhattan Island and Prince Edward Island are not very much

alike, they are still islands. Emily's father was dying of bad lungs, and so was mine. Emily had some dreadful relative, and so did I. She had a hard time in school, and she also understood that there's more to life than just the things that can be explained by encyclopedias and facts. Facts alone are not adequate. I love Emily.[2]

An Early Author

The home was always filled with people, usually artists of some sort, and their creativity clearly inspired Madeleine. "When I was five, I wrote my first story then about a little g-r-u-l—that's how I spelled 'girl' at the time. Spellcheck and I don't always agree!"[3] By the age of seven she had decided that she wanted to be famous some day. However, she didn't know what form of art she would choose because she loved music and acting almost as much as writing.

Music fascinated Madeleine as much as words, if not more. She loved all forms of classical music, but particularly Johann Sebastian Bach, and she loved to listen to the melodies and how they wove together. For her, words did much the same thing, weaving themselves into stories, and carrying emotion and energy through their tone. Poetry, of course, enthralled her, as it was a melding of music and words. In fifth grade, she won a poetry contest, but her teacher accused her of cheating and stealing the poem, saying Madeleine wasn't bright enough to have written it. Madeleine's mother then brought in several of the poems and stories Madeleine had written at home, proving Madeleine's creativity and writing skill. The next year the Camps transferred Madeleine to a different school, where her teacher actually encouraged her writing.

Fortunately for Madeleine, her parents loved the arts and loved to share them with her. Their home was filled with books of all sorts, and the Camps read aloud to each other every night. Some nights they read poetry, other nights fiction, and sometimes they read essays, treatises, or nonfiction works on serious topics. These nightly readings influenced Madeleine, both by giving her strong narrative models and by educating her on people, philosophy, and theology. She tried writing her first novel in fifth grade.

Relocating

When Madeleine was twelve years old, the Camps moved to Europe. Madeleine claimed years later that her father's lungs had been damaged by mustard gas during World War I (1914–1918), and had bothered him ever since. In the winter of 1930, he came down with pneumonia, and his doctors urged him to leave New York. So Camp moved his family to the French Alps, hoping the clear mountain air would be easier on him. While there, Madeleine attended Chatelard, an English boarding school in Montreaux, Switzerland. She hated the experience. The students were called by numbers, rather than by their names, and her classmates mispronounced her name when they did use it. Years later, Madeleine's first novel, *The Small Rain* (1945), would draw on some of these early experiences.

In 1932, after two years in Europe, the Camps moved back to the United States. Madeleine's grandmother, Caroline Hallows L'Engle Barnett, known as Dearma, was gravely ill, and the Camps moved to Jacksonville, Florida, to be near her. Shortly thereafter, Madeleine, who was about fifteen, was sent to Ashley Hall, a boarding school in Charleston, South Carolina. She did quite well there, particularly in English. This was the first time Madeleine was truly happy. She was making friends and had teachers who liked her and who treated her well. Madeleine took part in plays from 1935 to 1936, and was on the student council, where she was even student council president. She relished her time at Ashley Hall, which may be why many of her young heroines are the age she was while there. Like her, they stand poised on the brink of discovering who they really are, and who they can be.

Madeleine was seventeen and a senior at Ashley Hall when her father passed away of pneumonia. Not surprisingly, many of her books have dealt with the theme of death, particularly with children and young adults coming to terms with the death of a loved one. In her first novel, *The Small Rain*, for example, teenage Katherine Forrester has just lost her mother, just as teenage Madeleine lost her father.

L'Engle has commented in interviews that she did not have an easy childhood. Her parents loved her, but half the time they were too busy with their own lives to pay her much attention. When they did notice her, they fought over her, each vying for her attention. And she had little support from teachers or classmates while growing up. This only seems to have made her a stronger person, however. As she remarked once, "I was a solitary only child in New York City, so I spent a lot of time in my little back room writing, reading, being, thinking, wondering."[4] Madeleine decided early on that courage was crucial, particularly the courage to be herself. She often tells people to be brave and to do what they think they should do, regardless of whether it's expected or even desired. She encourages her fans to be open to new ideas and prepared for change, and to embrace their own strengths and be proud of their own personality.

Familiar Experiences

Most of L'Engle's books have young female protagonists, and she freely admits that she draws upon her own experiences to create them and to make them feel real. Meg, the main character in *A Wrinkle in Time* and *A Wind in the Door* (1973), is very much like Madeleine at that age (Meg is fourteen in *A Wrinkle in Time* and fifteen in *A Wind in the Door*), but with a few differences. "Of course I'm Meg. I made her good at arithmetic and bad at English, and I was good at English and bad at arithmetic. And I didn't have any brothers or sisters so I gave her three brothers. You can do that if you're a writer."[5] Meg is brilliant but misunderstood. She is not at all popular, in part because she is not very outgoing. Madeleine modestly denies the brilliance, but the other details certainly fit her childhood years. And, through her novels, L'Engle works out how a gifted but unconfident child can learn to become more confident, more outgoing, and more independent, and also how such a child can build lasting relationships with his or her family members and with other children.

L'Engle also focuses her books upon the issue of family, drawing from her own upbringing. As a child, Madeleine had no siblings, but she did have energetic, active, and creative parents. Her father was often distant, both physically and emotionally, and many of her characters have the same unsatisfying relationship with one or both parents. But Madeleine did still love her father and knew that he returned her love as well as he could. As Meg tells the Man with the Red Eyes in *A Wrinkle in Time*, "Didn't you ever have a father yourself? You don't want him for a reason. You want him because he's your father."[6] Madeleine also had uncles, aunts, cousins, and grandparents, and heard stories about a variety of other relatives. The person she heard the most about was Mado, whose long, full life had been filled with adventure and drama. Madeleine's namesake had gone from the riches of the Spanish court to the poverty of the post-World War I era, and she had handled herself with grace and generosity throughout. No one in the family had anything but good to say about her. Nor could anyone remember Mado saying anything bad about others. She had always been a lovely, soft-spoken, compassionate woman, but no one had missed noticing her wit or her strong will. Madeleine admired her great-grandmother considerably, and in many ways patterned herself after the woman, striving to be kind and generous, to know who she was, and never to let anyone tell her what to do.

Religious Roots

Madeleine's parents were Episcopalian, and Madeleine grew up not only going to church but also hearing about various religious figures. Her parents were as likely to read about a saint or a Christian minister as they were to read a novel, so the nighttime readings taught Madeleine many things about their faith and the other faiths of the world. But Madeleine's fierce independence made her uncomfortable with churches, and even then she resisted having anyone, minister or otherwise, tell her what she should feel and how she should respond. This attitude also appears throughout her books, where the children often discover that they are best served by ignoring tradition and finding individual methods to reach their goals.

Though Madeleine's parents read the Bible to her, they approached it as a storybook rather than as scripture. She was never told to take the stories literally, but rather to treat them as larger truths and valuable lessons. This distinction between truth and fact is one that has stayed with L'Engle for the rest of her life, and appears in many of her books, both fiction and nonfiction. At the same time, her appreciation for symbols and myths stems from this early familiarity with the Bible. Years later, this interest would actually get L'Engle in trouble with many more traditional Christians who felt she was using symbols inappropriately or that she was using symbols that no proper Christian would ever mention. But to L'Engle these symbols are only important for what they represent at the time. In many cases, she saw symbols that had been poorly used by others, or attached to negative notions because one person used them that way. By using them again in a more positive way, L'Engle attempted to restore these symbols to their proper place, and make them worthwhile once again. For example, L'Engle often uses rainbows in her books. In *A Wrinkle in Time*, Meg and Calvin rest and heal on the planet Ixchel, which is named for the Mayan goddess of the rainbow and patron of medicine. In the Bible, the rainbow symbolized God's covenant with Noah, and a renewal of faith and hope. But many people today see the rainbow as a New Age symbol rather than a Christian one. That is, the rainbow represents wide-ranging beliefs and practices. By naming the planet Ixchel, L'Engle reclaims the idea of the rainbow as a Christian image, offering Meg the chance for healing and recovery.

2 Theater and Romance

fter high school, L'Engle was accepted to Smith College, a prestigious women's college in Northampton, Massachusetts. She graduated cum laude (with honors) with a degree in English in 1941. Then she and three of her friends moved back to New York and got an apartment in Greenwich Village. Two of her friends were aspiring actresses. "I still wanted to be a writer," she recounts. "I always wanted to be a writer, but I had to pay the bills, so I went to work in the theater."[1] L'Engle decided upon theater because she had always enjoyed acting, and she also thought that theater would be good training for a writer. She wound up getting work with a small theater company. L'Engle also continued her schooling, attending classes at the

New School for Social Research from 1941 to 1942. She also wrote a play called *18 Washington Square, South: A Comedy in One Act*, which was produced in 1944.

It was during this time that L'Engle stopped using her father's name. She had nothing against him, or that side of her family, but she felt that her name was too unwieldy. "I only wanted two names and not three. And I was working in the theater to earn some money to write, and actress Eva Le Gallienne said, 'Why don't you just drop the Camp and use L'Engle?' I did. And I thought, well that's nice, it's a good name. It's more musical."[2]

A New Novelist

In 1945, while working in the theater, L'Engle wrote her first novel, entitled *The Small Rain*. Bernard Perry, an editor for Vanguard Press, had read some of the short stories she had published, and contacted her to ask if she had a novel she could send him. L'Engle was working on one at the time, and Perry offered to buy it when she'd finished it. The book is about a talented pianist, Katherine Forrester, and her life between the ages of ten and eighteen. It is set during the period between the First and Second World Wars (the 1920s and 1930s), and deals with Katherine's life and hardships. Katherine suffers a great deal in the novel, losing her mother at the start, rarely seeing her father, being shipped off to a Swiss boarding school, and experiencing several failed romances and one failed engagement. L'Engle drew on some of her own childhood experiences for the book, particularly the boarding school and the untimely loss of a parent. But her focus was on Katherine's personal growth and on how she managed to ultimately survive the many hardships she experienced.

Love in the Orchard

Almost two years before writing *The Small Rain*, L'Engle was cast in a production of Anton Chekhov's *The Cherry Orchard* (1904). This Russian play features a handful of men and women gathering on an old estate with a cherry orchard after the liberation of the serfs near the end of the nineteenth century. The play centers on Madame Ranevsky, who owns the estate but who is forced to auction it off to pay her debts. On the first day of rehearsal, L'Engle met a fellow actor named Hugh Franklin, who was from Tulsa, Oklahoma. As she tells it:

> When I went to the first rehearsal [of *The Cherry Orchard*] . . . I saw a very tall, thin young man with black hair and enormous, very blue eyes. I had never seen such eyes . . . The young man was introduced to me as Hugh Franklin, and I was told of some of his other featured

roles on Broadway . . . And there was no doubt that Hugh Franklin was a fine actor who brought a radiant and youthful idealism as well as talent to the role of Petya Trofimov . . . The rehearsal had started early, at ten in the morning, and broke at three. To my amazement, Petya Trofimov crossed the rehearsal hall to me and suggested that we get a bite to eat—we had not taken time out for lunch.

The rules of theatre etiquette were very different from the rules of debutante parties in Jacksonville, Florida, but they were rules, nevertheless. Women paid their own way. If a man picked up the tab it meant that something really serious was going on. Hugh and I sat over our hamburgers and milk shakes till nearly two in the morning. Then I paid my share of the tab and he walked me to the subway.

But we had talked for ten hours without noticing the time passing. I let myself into my apartment thinking elatedly, "I have met the man I want to marry." . . . Gone were doubts about the existence of real love. I wasn't anywhere near understanding it yet, but I was full of joy.[3]

Franklin felt the same way about L'Engle, and on January 26, 1946, they were married. The ceremony was small and sudden, and held in Chicago, Illinois, because they were currently on tour for *The Joyous Season*, a play written by Philip Barry in 1934. That year, Franklin and L'Engle also purchased a summer home, an old farmhouse near Goshen, in northwestern Connecticut. For the next year both of them were acting, but when their daughter, Josephine, was born in June 1947, Franklin persuaded L'Engle to give up her theatrical career. Instead she devoted herself to raising their daughter—determined not to be as distant to her child as her parents had been to her—and to writing full-time. Her second novel, *Ilsa*, was published by Vanguard Press in 1946, but L'Engle was never very happy with it. As she remembered years later, in her autobiographical work, entitled *Two-Part Invention: The Story of a Marriage* (1988):

> My second novel was accepted with enthusiasm. But alas, Bernard Perry was gone. There was nobody at Vanguard at that time to tell me that what I had submitted was an excellent first draft, but that my manuscript needed work—a lot of work. I have been blessed with editors who have pushed and prodded me, made me go back to the typewriter and revise. This second novel needed that kind of editorial nudging and didn't get it.[4]

The novel follows Henry Porcher, who falls in love with Ilsa Brandes from the moment he sees her, despite the fact that their parents cannot stand one another. The two maintain a platonic friendship for the rest of their lives, but despite his best efforts, Henry can neither win Ilsa's heart nor lose interest in her. This is one of the few novels where it's hard to see L'Engle in the characters, since she was in love with Hugh by the time she finished the book. Perhaps this is why she was never satisfied with how it turned out, and why it did not sell particularly well and was never reprinted, because she did not identify closely with the characters.

L'Engle's third novel, *And Both Were Young*, was published by Vanguard in 1949. It was her first book printed since she and Hugh married and since she had devoted herself fully to her writing. It is the story of Philippa "Flip" Hunter, a young woman from Connecticut who is stuck in a horrible boarding school. Philippa hates the school, and hates being separated from her beloved father, who is an artist. But she winds up making friends with a French boy named Paul Laurens, and slowly their friendship becomes a romance. As their love grows, Philippa becomes more confident, and she and Paul wind up secretly training for a ski tournament. In the end, Philippa decides that helping Paul is more important than winning, but winds up winning the tournament anyway. Philippa is the perfect example of L'Engle's heroines, a bright and pleasant young woman who feels out of place and too timid to assert herself.

And through the course of the novel, she becomes more confident and more secure, and eventually demonstrates to everyone that she has changed into a resourceful young woman. It is no coincidence that she is from Connecticut, and L'Engle drew heavily on her own recent trips there with Hugh to create that setting, while returning again to her school days for the portrayal of the unpleasant boarding school.

Growing Up

The 1940s brought many changes in L'Engle's life and many shifts in her perspective. She went from being a girl to being a woman, gained independence, and got her first job. She also began selling her novels. Then she fell in love, got married, and became a mother. And, finally, she began writing full-time. Her heroines are often the same age as she was when she graduated from Smith, or within a few years of that, because it is during these years that they determine their true selves and decide what path their lives will take. For L'Engle, as for many others, the 1940s were a time of great change, and her faith and her relationships with friends and family are what successfully saw her through that difficult decade.

L'Engle's religious beliefs also changed during this decade. Her parents had both been

Episcopalians, and had raised her to believe in God's unconditional love. But even as a child L'Engle had been uncomfortable with restrictions and with such rigid concepts of God. Her time in the Anglican boarding school in Switzerland only made matters worse. Then, while she was in high school, L'Engle's father died, and her church told her not to grieve because he had gone to a better place. While she did believe that he might be somewhere better now, and without pain, at the same time L'Engle was angry at her church for ordering her to suppress her emotions.

During her first year at Smith College, L'Engle decided that she was fed up with churches, and, in fact, with all organized religion. She did not attend church or belong to any formal religious community during her college years, or those first years in New York. Franklin had been raised as a Baptist since birth, but no longer believed in his church either. The two agreed not to join any congregations. L'Engle did occasionally attend Mass, but she went to several different churches so that no one could try to claim her as one of their regular members. The Bible remained very important to her, as did faith in general, but L'Engle no longer trusted others to interpret them for her. Instead, she was determined to study and pray and learn for herself.

Then, in 1951, L'Engle produced her fourth novel, *Camilla Dickinson*. Fifteen-year-old Camilla falls in love for the first time, with her best friend's brother, Frank Rowan. At the same time, however, Camilla's parents are fighting, and they each try to claim attention and affection from Camilla. L'Engle used her own memories for that tense home life. Camilla also fights to assert her independence and to pursue her dreams of becoming an astronomer. The characters in many of these early novels would appear again much later in L'Engle's life, weaving their way through other books as she began to tie many of her stories together.

By the time *Camilla Dickinson* was published, L'Engle was pregnant with her second child, Josephine was four years old, and Franklin had grown tired of the hustle and bustle of city life. Their world was about to change, and not necessarily for the better.

3 Mother and Wife

For several years, Franklin and L'Engle had lived in New York together. Franklin had continued to work in theater. L'Engle stayed at home, took care of their baby daughter, and wrote novels. But in 1952, they decided that they were tired. New York was a fun, exciting city, but it was also loud, busy, and dirty. That had been fine when Franklin and L'Engle had been young and single, and even when they had been newlyweds. But now they were parents, and were expecting their second child. Franklin was also tired of being on the road, and away from his wife and child. They wanted a quieter, simpler life.

The Franklins had bought a farmhouse in northwestern Connecticut the same year they'd gotten married, and spent the summers there, plus occasional weekends and short vacations. But now they decided to move there for good. Franklin renounced the theater, and the family packed their belongings and gave up their life in the city.

Their new home was a large, old, white farmhouse, which they had named Crosswicks. Crosswicks was the name of the New Jersey farm where L'Engle's father had grown up. This Crosswicks was near the town of Goshen, but not actually in town. The area around it was farmland, used mainly for raising dairy cows. It was a very pretty place. L'Engle says: "Oh, the beauty of the mountains, the loveliness of no city lights, no noises at night. It was a very safe place to start off raising our kids. We were outside of Goshen, a dairy farm village with about 200 people. It's a gentle view, old mountains that were worn down by time and rain and wind, gentle mountains."[1]

Of course, now that Franklin was no longer acting, they needed some other way to earn a living. So they bought a run-down general store in Goshen itself, fixed it up, and became shopkeepers. Their second child, a son named Bion (whose namesake was L'Engle's grandfather, Bion Barnett), was born shortly after the move, on March 24, 1952. Between two children, a farmhouse, and a store, Franklin and L'Engle had their hands full.

Still, it was nice to be out of the tension of New York, and away from all the distractions that a big city has to offer.

In 1955, one of the Franklins' closest friends died suddenly. A year later, his wife passed away, leaving their seven-year-old daughter, Maria, on her own. Franklin and L'Engle felt the loss of their friends keenly, and couldn't bear the thought of Maria being sent away to strangers, so they adopted her themselves. Now their family was complete.

Country Writing

L'Engle continued to write, of course. She couldn't really stop herself. It was not easy to find the time, however. She recounts that "helping to build up, participate in the life of a small, but very active community, run a large farmhouse and raise three small children is the perfect way not to write a book. I did manage to write at night. Writing is, for me, an essential function, like sleeping and breathing."[2]

The first book she wrote after the move was *Meet the Austins* (1960), which was to become one of her most successful and best-loved novels. This pleasant book introduces the Austin family, who was featured in several later books as well. In fact, after the Murrys and the related O'Keefes, the Austins are L'Engle's most commonly seen characters. The

Austins deal with the loss of a favorite uncle, similar to the way the Franklins were dealing with the loss of Maria's parents, who were so close to the Franklins that they were basically an aunt and uncle to Josephine and Bion. *Meet the Austins* parallels the Franklins' own life in the country, and its scenes of communal life are drawn to some extent from L'Engle's experiences at Crosswicks and in Goshen.

Unfortunately, although she was writing novels, L'Engle was not selling them. Both *Meet the Austins* and another novel, *A Winter's Love* (1957), were rejected by several publishers. With each rejection, L'Engle became more dejected, and her confidence as a writer plummeted. She actually got to the point where "I used to put the kids to bed and take my dogs and walk them down the long dirt road in front of my house and cry my eyes out."[3] She even tried to quit writing, but found that writing had become essential for her. "I couldn't stop writing and I kept on writing. I had no choice. I might never get published, but I had to keep writing."[4]

L'Engle did eventually sell *A Winter's Love* in 1957, and in 1960 she finally sold *Meet the Austins*. They were the only two complete novels she wrote during the Franklins' time at Crosswicks. Part of that was because she was very busy. She now had three children to raise, and was helping Franklin with the store, which proved surprisingly successful. But the other reason was because she had become less sure of herself as a writer.

Too Quiet

L'Engle often looks back upon the eight years at Crosswicks as a low point in her life, or at least in her writing. She was happy with her family, and did love the quiet of the countryside, but both she and Franklin began to feel less than whole. She missed her writing, he missed the theater, and both of them missed the excitement of the city. They had also become part of the Goshen community, and slowly realized that small-town life can be just as tense as big-city life. There were fewer distractions, but the existing ones often became more noticeable as a result. And the store, initially a hobby and a way to supplement their savings, had grown into a real business, which brought headaches of its own. They were also appalled at the lack of education available for their children. Most of the neighbors' children, including the teenagers, couldn't read, and many had never even seen books before going to school. All of these factors built upon each other, and in 1960 the Franklins decided they'd had enough. They sold the store, packed up again, and moved back to New York. According to L'Engle, "We got back just in time."[5]

Although she did not write much during those years, the time at Crosswicks may have been more important than L'Engle herself realized. She began the first of her larger series, introduced the first of her major families, and established settings and characters she would build upon for years to come. But more important, she had time to think during that period. Although she didn't write as much, L'Engle never stopped looking at the world, never stopped considering it, and never stopped asking questions. And, with fewer distractions, she started finding some answers. After they left Crosswicks, L'Engle began writing again, and at a furious pace. Her books seemed to appear almost magically, one after the other. It was as if she had finally worked out several important issues, and could now build stories upon them whenever she chose. Without that time at Crosswicks, and those experiences, L'Engle might not have written her next novel, which was to become her greatest masterpiece.

A Love of Science

L'Engle also found some time to read while at Crosswicks, both stories to her children and books for herself. One of the topics she began to study was science. She had never been very good at math as a child, and had only the basic science education from her school days. But science fascinated her. More accurately, L'Engle was fascinated by the possibilities that science presented. Scientists were discovering new things every day, from mathematical models of the universe to microbes that help humans fight infection. And with each new discovery, L'Engle saw new questions and new answers as well. She loved the fact that science forced her to shift her perspective and see everything in a new way. Part of that was a matter of scale—the world looks very different to a microbe, or to a star, than it does to a human being.

All of these thoughts whirled about in L'Engle's head. She didn't understand every bit of science she read, but that didn't bother her. "I have no science background," she admitted once, "But I read a lot about particle physics and quantum mechanics, and I have a few scientist friends who will let me pick their brains. I came across the word 'tesseracts' in a science article and got kind of fascinated by it."[6] She could see what they were saying, what they claimed they had discovered, and that was all she needed. Once she knew about mitochondria or tesseracts, she could let the ideas swim about and her imagination would do the rest. For L'Engle, science was simply a stepping-off point. She found the steps themselves fascinating, but what she really wanted to do was get wherever they were leading her.

L'Engle began weaving these same notions into her books. Many of her later novels contain scientific elements woven through the plot. And, thanks to her easy style and her focus upon the bigger picture, L'Engle was able to teach children science without distracting them from the story. In fact, many children learned the science she offered without realizing they were learning at all. She had a way of making even difficult concepts easy to understand, and the fact that it was other children explaining it made her readers more likely to pay attention and more apt to remember. To this day, many people understand the concept of tesseracts because they read *A Wrinkle in Time*, and mitochondria and cell functions because they read *A Wind in the Door*.

4 A New Wrinkle

Although the Franklins had decided to leave Crosswicks and move back to New York, they didn't take a direct route. Instead, they spent ten weeks traveling across the country, camping at various spots along the way. While on this trip, L'Engle had an idea for a new novel. This one was different from her previous stories. It still had a young female protagonist who was bright but misunderstood. It still focused on family, and had religious themes. But it had two new elements as well: science and fantasy. Even L'Engle herself wasn't sure how everything would fit together. But she was excited by the possibilities.

The Franklins returned to New York in the winter of 1960, and rented an eight-room apartment on the ninth floor of a building on West End Avenue, on Manhattan's Upper West Side, facing the Hudson River. Franklin returned to the theater, and L'Engle went back to school, doing graduate work at Columbia University from 1960 to 1961.

Publication Woes

In 1960, L'Engle also completed the novel she had begun a year earlier. It was called *A Wrinkle in Time*, and was easily her most ambitious work so far. L'Engle was pleased with the results: "I knew it was a good book when I finished it, I was very excited by it. I knew it was the best thing I'd ever done."[1]

Unfortunately, publishers didn't agree. She had given the novel to a literary agent, and he sent it to publisher after publisher. Each one rejected it. Many sent her form-letter replies. These impersonal responses are usually reserved for novels that have no redeeming value. For L'Engle, who had already published six novels, it was an insult. She didn't understand why no one seemed to want the novel she was certain was her best. These days, most publishers can't understand what happened either, as L'Engle recalls: "I can't tell you how many publishers have said 'Oh

I wish I'd gotten my hands on that book' and I say 'You did.' One publisher didn't believe me until I sent him a copy of the rejection slip."[2]

Finally, after trying more than forty publishers, they gave up. Her agent sent the manuscript back, and L'Engle admitted that no one was going to buy it. Fortunately, that Christmas her mother was visiting, and one day L'Engle threw a tea party for her mother and her old friends. One of the friends was part of a small writing group, along with a man named John Farrar. Farrar was part of a small publishing house, Farrar, Straus & Giroux, and the friend insisted that L'Engle meet with him. Though she didn't expect it to help, L'Engle agreed to meet him, and she brought her manuscript along. During the meeting, Farrar told her that he'd read her first novel, *The Small Rain*, and had liked it. He agreed to read *A Wrinkle in Time*. He loved it, so he bought it. The book had finally found a home more than two years after L'Engle had finished it.

A Wrinkle in Time wasted no time proving all those other publishers wrong. It was released in 1962, and in 1963 it won the prestigious Newbery Medal (Named for John Newbery, an eighteenth-century bookseller, the Newbery Medal is awarded yearly by the Association for Library Service to

Children, a division of the American Library Association, to the writer of the most distinguished contribution to American literature for children). *A Wrinkle in Time* also won the Sequoyah Award, the Lewis Carroll Shelf Award, and was a runner-up for the Hans Christian Andersen Award. More important, *A Wrinkle in Time* was an instant hit with children everywhere, and has remained one of the most popular children's books of all time.

Wrinkles of Confusion

One of the problems L'Engle had selling her manuscript for *A Wrinkle in Time* was the question of age. Several publishers, after reading the manuscript, had asked L'Engle what age she had been writing for. She didn't really have an answer for that. Some writers do set out to tell a story for children, or a novel for adults, but L'Engle doesn't really think that way. She writes the stories and then lets her agent or the publishers figure out what age group will read it. But with *A Wrinkle in Time*, the intended readership was even more confusing. The book had clear elements of fantasy, which suggested a younger audience. The main character was in her early teens, which also indicated that it was a children's book. It also had a female protagonist, whereas science-fiction books up to then had always had male main characters. But, as L'Engle responded years later, "I'm a female. Why would I give all the best ideas to a male?"[3]

There was also the matter of the science content, which many adults had trouble understanding, and the fantastical elements. Most people thought those two elements could not be mixed. L'Engle didn't see a problem with it. "Another assumption was that science and fantasy don't mix. Why not? We live in a fantastic universe, and subatomic particles and quantum mechanics are even more fantastic than the macrocosm. Often the only way to look clearly at this extraordinary universe is through fantasy, fairy tale, myth."[4] When it bought the book, Farrar, Straus & Giroux didn't even have a juvenile section and it didn't normally do fantasy novels, but John Farrar was too impressed not to buy it. The company started a new juvenile line and made *A Wrinkle in Time* the first release. It was the right choice—despite the adult topics, *A Wrinkle in Time* is easily accessible, and children immediately identify with the characters.

The book introduces the Murrys, L'Engle's most popular family. Meg, the teenage protagonist, is everything L'Engle herself was at that age—brilliant, awkward, shy, and a bit angry at the world. Meg's mother takes care of her and her three brothers because her father vanished some time ago. Meg still misses him, and her youngest brother, Charles Wallace, insists that their father, a physicist who researches time travel, needs help. Meg agrees to go with Charles Wallace to find him. This is when the novel gets strange. Meg, Charles Wallace, and Calvin O'Keefe, their new friend, meet a peculiar old woman named Mrs. Whatsit, who uses a tesseract to take them to another world called Camazotz. (A tesseract is a fourth-dimensional object that moves through the fifth dimension, creating a wrinkle through space and time.) On Camazotz, where everything appears exactly alike and where everyone must abide by the rules of conformity and uniformity, she introduces the three children to her colleagues, Mrs. Who and Mrs. Which. They tell Meg and Charles Wallace that their father is being held prisoner by a creature, a disembodied brain, known as IT. Only Meg and Charles, with Calvin's help, can rescue him, and stop IT's evil plans.

On its surface, *A Wrinkle in Time* is about two children trying to rescue their father. But it is really a tale of good versus evil, of individuality versus conformity, of courage versus fear, and love versus hate, for in the end it is Meg's love for her brother that triumphs over IT. The book also emphasizes the importance of family, as most of L'Engle's books do, and the value of individuality. Meg and Charles Wallace are not normal children. Meg is a gawky, moody twelve-year-old who fights with the school bully. Meg wants to be more like everyone else in school. Four-year-old Charles Wallace is extraordinarily bright and has second sight, the power of foreseeing future events. Neither of them fits in well, but the siblings' parents have encouraged them to be who they really are, not who everyone else thinks they should be. Meg and Calvin escape Camazotz with Mr. Murry, but Charles remains behind, possessed by the evil IT. Meg realizes that only she can save her brother, and she travels back to Camazotz to rescue him. In the end, the Murry family and Calvin are reunited on Earth. Many critics have called the book an allegory about love and compassion versus hate, anger, and pride. It is an allegory about evil, and evil's power over the human soul. The book is also an allegory of individuality, where Meg learns the value of her differences from others and accepts her uniqueness.

Following the Murrys

L'Engle published several more books after *A Wrinkle in Time*, and her fame grew with each novel. It took several years, however, before she returned to the Murrys. In 1965, she wrote *The Arm of the Starfish*, which includes Calvin and Meg, now married with children of their own. In 1973, however, L'Engle wrote *A Wind in the Door*, which is a true sequel to *A Wrinkle in Time*. It features Meg and Charles Wallace again, and picks up their story from where the first book left off. Like *A Wrinkle in Time*, *A Wind in the Door* involves fantastic journeys and living beings that do not exist in our world. In this story, Charles Wallace has become strangely ill. To save him, Meg has to shrink herself down to microscopic size and enter his bloodstream, where she meets mitochondria, farandolae, and other tiny beings who live in a world of their own. Meg's boyfriend, Calvin, and Mr. Jenkins, the school principal, are Meg's companions in the adventure. Just as with *A Wrinkle in Time*, *A Wind in the Door* is often considered an allegory. The novel deals with the question of sickness, but particularly sickness of the soul and of the spirit. Charles Wallace is being consumed by a darkness from within that is fed by doubt, hate, and despair.

Years later, L'Engle wrote a third book about Meg and Charles Wallace. In *A Swiftly Tilting Planet*, published in 1978, fifteen-year-old Charles Wallace works with a unicorn, Gaudior, to save the world from nuclear war. But in order to stop the menacing South American dictator Madog Branzillo, who has threatened to destroy the universe in twenty-four hours by using an atomic bomb, Charles Wallace goes back in time and experiences the lives of four people from different eras. Each of these people is part of the modern-day dictator's past, and by becoming them, Charles Wallace can use that past to change the present and protect the future. This novel, even more than most of L'Engle's others, deals with the issue of family and how important family can be to a person's development. *A Swiftly Tilting Planet* won the American Book Award in 1980.

These three novels, *A Wrinkle in Time*, *A Wind in the Door*, and *A Swiftly Tilting Planet*, are often referred to as the Time Trilogy, and are L'Engle's best-known works. In 1986, she wrote a fourth book, *Many Waters*, which features Meg and Charles Wallace's brothers, the twins Sandy and Dennys. The twins accidentally get transported back to the time of the biblical Great Flood, and have to find a way home before the entire world is washed away.

Sometimes this book is included with the other three in a set called the Time Quartet, but *Many Waters* lacks the scientific elements of the other three, and seems less focused on the questions of good, evil, and conformity. *Many Waters* does involve time travel, however, and does deal with issues of family, and with two youths' coming-of-age.

Chronos and Kairos

A Wrinkle in Time was the first of L'Engle's novels to involve things beyond this world. She had been wrestling with these concepts for years, however. This was simply the first time she had worked them into one of her books. In particular, L'Engle had begun to think about chronos versus kairos. Chronos is time in the traditional sense. Seconds, minutes, hours, and days are part of chronos. It is the time of the real world.

Kairos, on the other hand, is idealized time. It is perfect time, or God's time. Kairos is the opportune moment and cannot be measured because it is not part of this world. It is beyond the world.

All of L'Engle's previous novels are based on chronos. They are set in the real world, and deal with realistic people, realistic settings, and realistic issues. But *A Wrinkle in Time* is set in the time of kairos. It steps away from our reality, and moves to a place that does not exist. Here L'Engle could talk about anything and invent new terms to describe what she meant. Time no longer mattered; it could no longer be measured. Everything was filled with possibility because nothing was bound. (In other words, using watches and clocks restricts our activities and puts boundaries on our world. But living without a clear sense of time makes us free again.)

After *A Wrinkle in Time*, L'Engle did write several more books in chronos time, mainly the rest of the Austin series. But she also wrote several more books in kairos time, including the rest of the Time Quartet. She divided her writing between the real world and the worlds of possibility. And her readers learned to appreciate both but discovered that the kairos novels had more to say and more to teach. This may be why the Time Quartet and the other kairos novels are her more popular works. They step beyond our reality and tell a larger, more universal story, one that touches upon worlds as well as individuals.

A Better World

L'Engle posed some questions about fate and destiny when she wrote *A Wrinkle in Time*. She was looking for a world she could believe in, one that made more sense than the real world. After all, she thought of this novel right after leaving Crosswicks, and in many ways the nearly ten years the Franklins spent in Connecticut didn't make any sense to her. Many of her previous characters had felt out of place and had searched for a way to fit in, or at least a way to feel more comfortable with themselves. But with *A Wrinkle in Time* L'Engle suggested that perhaps the problem was with the world itself, not with the characters. Perhaps they didn't feel right because this world was not where they belonged. Or the world simply wasn't what it should have been. In *A Wrinkle in Time*, the evil has begun enveloping the world, and taints everything it touches. L'Engle believed this, but she also believed that the world could be made into a different place. Love, compassion, hope, and courage were the keys to this transformation. Many of her earlier novels focused on these same elements, but only on a personal level. With *A Wrinkle in Time*, L'Engle shifted the scale. Her novels were still about characters trying to make sense of their lives. At the same time they had to save the world from itself.

5 Life Goes On

With *A Wrinkle in Time*, L'Engle went from being a moderately successful author to being an award-winning novelist. Over the next forty years, she wrote at least a book a year, and often more. Also, she and Franklin had not been idle otherwise.

After they returned to New York, Franklin went back into acting in theater. He later switched to television, however, and eventually became a soap opera star. Franklin played the character of Dr. Charles Tyler on the daytime soap opera *All My Children*. He is still remembered for that role.

L'Engle herself got a job again, this time in teaching. Over the next six years she taught at St. Hilda's and St. Hugh's, both Anglican schools in New York City. She also spent several summers on the faculty of the University of Indiana in Bloomington, teaching writing. In 1965, L'Engle accepted a post as writer-in-residence and librarian at the Cathedral Church of St. John the Divine in New York City. Which title she uses depends on what she's doing that day: "It depends from day-to-day on what they want to call me. I do keep the library collection—largely theology, philosophy, a lot of good reference books—open on a volunteer basis."[1] She still holds that job today, and spends as much of her time as she can in their small library, organizing, filing, and writing.

The Journals

In the 1970s, L'Engle began writing something new. She was still writing her children's novels, but she also started writing a new series. This series, called the Crosswicks Journals, after their farmhouse, was all about her life. It was nonfiction and was meant more for adults than for children, though as always L'Engle let the work choose its audience.

In 1986, Hugh Franklin died after a long battle with cancer. He and L'Engle had been married for forty years. The third and final volume of the Crosswicks Journals, *Two-Part Invention: The Story of a Marriage*, details their marriage from beginning to end. Many of L'Engle's readers recognized the same focus on death they had seen in her novels over the years, but this time it was about her real life, and that of her beloved Hugh.

The journals are not depressing, however. L'Engle has dealt with death since losing her father. She has learned something very important about grief over the years: "We can help each other bear it. Not just by caring, by making it bearable because we care—though that helps . . . Mado did it by prayer. She took people's pain and she bore some of it for them."[2] L'Engle's journals talk about many things, including how to live a meaningful life. By talking about her own experiences, L'Engle shows that people can overcome grief, anger, resentment, and conformity. She leads by example.

Religious Texts

L'Engle also started writing more openly religious books. She wrote several novels based on biblical stories, including a novel called *Sold into Egypt: Joseph's Journey into Human Being* (1989). And she wrote books about religion, including *Walking on Water: Reflections on Faith and Art* (1980).

But these books did not make L'Engle more popular with Christian readers. If anything, more Christians disliked her because L'Engle talked in her books about how it is OK to be angry with God, to question God, and to argue with

God's decisions. This is not what most Christians are taught. Churches teach that people should obey God and accept that God knows best. But L'Engle didn't believe that. She did agree that God was amazing and wonderful, but she also said that God could make mistakes, or misunderstand. And she felt that it was her duty to correct him when he was wrong. As she explained once, "I've never been afraid to be angry with God. When I wrote *The Summer of the Great-Grandmother*, the book of my mother's last year, many people wrote, 'I didn't know I was allowed to be angry at God.' What kind of a God is it that you cannot honestly be angry with?"[3] It was also her right to demand an explanation. L'Engle didn't think she was the only one who could do this. She suggested that everyone should be able to question God that way.

Reading L'Engle's journals and religious discussions shows how life and faith have influenced her writing. Her journals talk about her relationships with her parents, her husband, and her children. They show how important family and family communication are to L'Engle. They also show how family life can affect every aspect of your world, especially your confidence. Her religious discussions show her interest in questioning everything, particularly authority and destiny, and in looking for answers. Her novels are simply ways to demonstrate those questions, and to help other people ask as well.

The Silver Screen

L'Engle's books have stayed immensely popular over the years. Many people have tried to turn them into movies or television shows, particularly *A Wrinkle in Time*. But L'Engle resisted every attempt and turned down every offer. She felt that the screenwriters never really understood the novel, and so they couldn't possibly turn it into a good script.

Recently, however, she changed her mind. She allowed Disney to turn *A Wrinkle in Time* into a three-hour movie. It aired on ABC's *Wonderful World of Disney* on Monday, May 10, 2004. L'Engle said afterward that "I expected it to be bad, and it is."[4] Fans had mixed opinions. Many hated it because the movie altered several details and featured updated language. Others felt that it captured the important elements, particularly the three children and the larger themes. Translating a book into a movie is always difficult, but it becomes harder when the book has fantastical elements. The film's producers used special effects to create the tesseract, Mrs. Whatsit's other form (when she changes to a horse with a human torso), and the rest of the strange, otherworldly sights and actions. But somehow they seem less real when caught on film. Readers can see the effects in their imagination and each one sees something different. That makes it more personal and more effective. The film has set effects for each event, so everyone sees exactly the same thing, but for most people the special effect does not match the image in their imagination.

The movie won the 2003 Best Feature Film Award at the Toronto Children's Film Festival. It was filmed in Canada, mainly in Vancouver and Whistler. It isn't a word-for-word adaptation, and does change some scenes, but stays faithful to the intent of the book and the basics of the plot and the characters.

A Ring of Endless Light (1980) premiered on the Disney Channel on August 23, 2002, as a made-for-TV movie. This adaptation from the book was less faithful and cut out most of the darker elements from the book's plot, replacing them with a plot about saving the dolphins from villainous fishermen. Producer-director Greg Beeman worked on both films, and he and L'Engle reportedly became friends in between.

L'Engle was also the subject of a half-hour documentary called *Madeleine L'Engle: Star*Gazer*, produced and directed by Martha Wheelock and distributed by Ishtar Films in 1988. This short author profile shows L'Engle speaking with a class of sixth-graders, preaching at the Cathedral Church of St. John the Divine, discussing her philosophies on life, and playing her piano at Crosswicks.

On Her Own

After Franklin's death, L'Engle continued her writing. She worked at the Cathedral of St. John the Divine whenever she was in New York. But she traveled often, doing book signings and lectures and teaching at colleges. Now that she was famous, L'Engle could write any type of book she wanted. "I've always believed that there is no subject that is taboo for the writer," she said once. "It is how it is written that makes a book acceptable, as a work of art, or unacceptable and pornographic."[5] Now she was able to enjoy that artistic freedom. She still wrote children's books, journals, and religious discussions. But now she also started writing books of essays and poems. She even wrote a picture book called *The Other Dog* in 2001.

In 1999, two major events changed L'Engle's life. First, in February, her first great-grandchild, Konstantinos John Voiklis, was born. L'Engle was thrilled. She had stayed close to her three children over the years. Josephine Jones is a psychotherapist who resides in northwestern Connecticut. Josephine's children, Léna Roy, and Charlotte and

Edward Jones, now help L'Engle with her business and correspondence. Maria Rooney, who grew up to be a professional photographer, even helped her write several books. Bion, who had hoped to be a writer and who married a doctor, Laurie, ran Crosswicks, Ltd., the company L'Engle had formed during the late 1960s to handle her business affairs and oversee her intellectual properties. L'Engle kept the apartment on the Upper West Side, and her children and grandchildren were always stopping by. And now she was a great-grandmother.

The second event was less pleasant. On December 17, her son, Bion, died. He was only forty-seven years old. Bion had been ill for some time, and had suffered liver damage the year before, but his death was still unexpected. L'Engle was devastated. So were her fans. Bion had been more than Madeleine L'Engle's son—he had been the role model for Rob Austin, and also for Charles Wallace Murry, two of her most beloved characters.

Truths and Untruths

To make matters worse, several years later, in April 2004, the *New Yorker* ran an article by Cynthia Zarin about L'Engle. In the article, Zarin stated that Bion's death was caused by the long-term effects of alcoholism. L'Engle refused to comment on the article.

Zarin also stated that L'Engle had not been totally accurate about her own history. According to the article, the details in L'Engle's journals and biographies were distorted. Some of them were even completely false. L'Engle had never claimed that the Crosswicks Journals were factual, however. She had admitted earlier that her Crosswicks Journals were not the same as her real-life journals. As a writer, she had modified the entries before publishing them. She cut scenes that didn't matter, rewrote other scenes, and modified details. She didn't consider this a lie because she hadn't claimed that every detail was real. And, for her, the stories were certainly true, even if they hadn't really happened. As she stated in her book *A Circle of Quiet* (1972):

> By the time I've finished a book I have no idea what in it is fabrication and what is actuality; and . . . that this holds true not only for novels but for most of my life. We do live, all of us, on many different levels, and for most artists the world of imagination is more real than the world of the kitchen sink.[6]

L'Engle has never claimed to be perfect. In fact, she always says she isn't perfect. No one is. She says she is trying to be good, and to be better, but of course she is flawed. The flaws are often what make people more interesting. None of her characters are perfect either. Even Meg and Charles Wallace Murry have their flaws—Meg is too quick to dismiss her own abilities, and Charles Wallace is too convinced of his own genius. They are both good people, and both brilliant, but they do have flaws. The flaws give them something to improve.

Health Concerns

L'Engle continued to write at least one book every year. Unfortunately, that has slowed more recently. In February 2002, she suffered a stroke. Although she recovered, it convinced her to slow down. Now L'Engle spends more time thinking and conversing, and less time touring and writing. In 2003, she received a pacemaker, which slowed her down even more. She has also had two hip operations, and now spends at least part of her time in a wheelchair. But L'Engle continues to work at the Cathedral Church of St. John the Divine. She still gives talks, and she still writes.

On November 17, 2004, twelve days before her eighty-sixth birthday, L'Engle had the honor of receiving the National Humanities Medal. This medal is awarded to individuals and organizations whose work has deepened the nation's understanding of the humanities. According to the National Endowment for the Humanities, which sponsors the award, L'Engle was cited for "her talent as a writer on spirituality and art and for her wonderful novels for young people. Her works inspire the imagination and reflect the creative spirit of America." Although L'Engle was in the hospital recuperating from a fall, her granddaughter Charlotte Jones was able to accept the medal from President George W. Bush in the Oval Office on L'Engle's behalf.

L'Engle is a gracious woman and cheerfully talks to people. If anything, she is more open now about her thoughts and feelings. Being old isn't so bad, she told *Newsweek* reporter Melinda Henneberger during an interview on May 7, 2004, because "I can say what I want, and I don't get punished for it."[7]

Some Perspective

L'Engle also still attends church. She goes to the All Angels Episcopal Church, on West Eightieth Street, and attends prayers every day at the cathedral as well. After all those years of disliking churches, she finally found a place that felt comfortable for her. L'Engle has said that she likes this church because the members know that they don't have all the answers. They also know that the church can't give them answers. It can only help them find answers for themselves. The other thing she likes is that the church does not tell her to hide her feelings. It encourages her to grieve when people die. This is the opposite of the churches she used to attend. When her father died, the church told L'Engle not to grieve because he had gone to a better place. She prefers the openness of her current church, and the support she gets from the other congregation members.

In 1996, L'Engle wrote a novel called *A Live Coal in the Sea*. The main character was Camilla Dickinson, the same Camilla from her fourth novel. In *A Live Coal in the Sea*, Camilla and her family try to overcome their differences. Many of those differences are caused by age. People from different generations just think differently. Madeleine L'Engle is now in her late eighties. She has lived through one World War. She is a great-grandmother. She has seen many things that younger people would never understand. But in *A Live Coal in the Sea*, she tries to bridge the gap between the generations.

6 The Writer's World

Some writers plot out their stories beforehand. They know everything that's going to happen. L'Engle doesn't work that way. She often doesn't know what a character will do until he or she does it. L'Engle doesn't tell her characters what to do. As she explained during an interview with María Ruiz Scaperlanda in May 2004:

> "I know my best work is unself-conscious. When I'm really writing," she explains in a bedtime-story voice, "I'm listening, and I'm not in control. That's when I finish and look back and say, 'I wrote that?'"[1]

The other thing L'Engle believes is that once an event has been written down, even she cannot change them. When she wrote *The Arm of the Starfish*, her son wanted her to change what happened:

> When I finished the final draft I read it out loud to my mother and my then ten-year-old son. When I got to the scene where Joshua is shot and killed, my son said, "Change it."
>
> "I can't change it," I said. "That's what happened."
>
> He said, "You're the writer. You can change it."
>
> "I can't change it. That's what happened."
>
> I didn't want Joshua to die, either. But that's what happened. If I tried to change it, I'd be deviating from the truth of the story.[2]

Listening to the Story

Every writer approaches writing differently. For L'Engle, writing is an act of prayer. She sees God as the primary creator of any art. Before writing, L'Engle sits quietly and prays. She opens herself up to God. She asks him to come to her and to write through her. According to L'Engle, all creativity is about letting the creative impulse guide you. You cannot control it. Trying to take control limits what you can do. "Artists of all disciplines must be willing to go into the dark, let go [of their] control, be surprised."[3] If you can let your imagination take over, the possibilities are endless.

Different writers also focus on different aspects. For some, stories are all about character. Others concentrate on dialogue. L'Engle focuses on the story. She loves her characters and wants to see what happens to them next. A few years ago she told an interviewer that she was working on a new adult novel, tentatively entitled *The Eye Begins to See*, about Meg Murry O'Keefe, a grandmother now in her fifties. L'Engle said that she was looking forward to seeing what Meg had been up to in the intervening years. According to L'Engle, a good story makes you want to find out what happens next, and a good storyteller can write so that you are interested in the story. Even the best story would be boring if it were poorly told. But a good storyteller can interest you in a mediocre story because she or he tells it so well.

She also believes that all writing tells a story. Her journals are stories. They are nonfiction, but they still tell the story of her own life, and she is still telling that story to her readers.

Story Choices

Another thing that makes L'Engle different from other writers is her audience. Most writers decide who they want to read their stories. But L'Engle doesn't decide who the audience will be. She speaks to children the same way she speaks to adults. And that makes her novels more accessible.

L'Engle does notice genre, however. She sometimes sets out to write a mystery, a fantasy novel, or a book of poems. And she does not like writing for the same genre twice in a row. She prefers to vary what she is writing to keep things more interesting. This is why she has written so many types of books. All of them discuss the same issues, but in very different ways. *A Wrinkle in Time*, *A Circle of Quiet*, and *The Summer of the Great- Grandmother* all talk about family, love, and strength, but they use different forms and different stories to illustrate the same points.

Truth Versus Fact

L'Engle's books do not always take place in the real world. Some of them occur in other times, like *Many Waters* does, or even on other planets, like the setting in *A Wrinkle in Time*. Yet they feel real. The characters are people we can understand. They are doing things we might do. And they are dealing with problems we have ourselves. For example, when Sandy and Dennys get thrown back in time in *Many Waters*, they're just trying to get home safely. The novels are true, even if they are not factual.

This is one of L'Engle's strongest beliefs. "Truth is what is true, and it's not necessarily factual," she explains. "Truth and fact are not the same thing. Truth does not contradict or deny facts, but it goes through and beyond facts."[4]

Facts are details you can confirm yourself. Twelve inches is a foot. This is a fact. If you get a ruler, you can see it. If you have forty-three cents in your pocket, that is a fact. Someone else could empty your pocket and count out the forty-three cents. You could close your eyes and pull out the money. You could put your pants in a drawer, and take them back out three weeks later. You still have forty-three cents in that pocket. That is a fact.

Most people think fact and truth are the same thing. If you say you have forty-three cents in your pocket, and you do, it is true. You told the truth. And it is a fact. But not all truths can be proven. Many are ideas, such as "love can conquer the world" or "anger never solved anything." Can you prove these things? Not the same way you can prove how much money you have in your pocket.

Truths, the way L'Engle uses the word, are larger notions. They are principles that guide our lives and shape the universe. But they are much bigger than we are. They involve emotions, time, and energy. They are not physical details. We cannot prove them to be the same every time. They are not factual.

When L'Engle writes a book, her goal is to ask questions. She hopes the book will help her find answers. But she does not want facts. She wants truths. Often, her books ask how good can overcome evil. Good and evil are abstract notions. A person can be evil, but evil itself has no one form. Neither does good. So how can good overcome evil? How can anyone even prove that good and evil exist? They are concepts, and cannot be proven with facts. So the answers have no facts either. According to *A Wrinkle in Time*, "Love can conquer hate." Love is good, and hate is evil. But we cannot prove this.

This is why Madeleine L'Engle's books still delight readers. *A Wrinkle in Time* was published in 1962, but readers today still enjoy it because it talks about issues that are still important. Meg and Charles Wallace are still people we like. We still want them to find their father. IT is still menacing. And Meg's growing self-confidence still shows us that we can be strong ourselves. Her realization that love can beat evil is still something we should all learn. It is still the truth. And, as L'Engle says, truth is more important. Truths are eternal. And so are the stories that share them.

Hard Work

L'Engle is a very diligent writer. Whenever she is anywhere near her word processor, she starts writing. She also edits constantly, but knowing what happens at the end of the story makes it easier for her to go back and revise the story, tighten it up, and make it read better. Sometimes the novel requires more substantial revisions. For example, when she was working on *Certain Women* (1992), L'Engle admitted in a 1991 interview with Shel Horowitz (posted on Frugalfun.com and excerpted in *Writer's Digest* in 1992) that:

> I'm on the fifth MAJOR revision . . . at this point. It started out to be a novel about King David's 8 wives. But I realized I could not put myself back 3,000 years in time. I had to have a 20th century point of view. So I had an 87 year old dying actor who had 8 wives, as did King David. He makes a lot of the similarities between their lives. King David is a role he's always wanted to play. The play never gets finished for a variety of reasons. I move from 3,000 years ago to the '40s to the '60s before Vietnam. So I've got a real technical challenge.[5]

Fortunately, L'Engle loves to write. Actually, she lives to write. She writes not because she chooses to, but because she feels she has to. It isn't something she can give up, even during those years when everything she wrote was rejected for publication. She also writes whenever she can and admits that she can get very unpleasant when she doesn't get enough time to write.

L'Engle loves words in general. She believes that a good vocabulary is very important for everyone, not just writers. As her character Katherine Forrester says in *The Small Rain*, "when you put something into words, it leads to so many other thoughts."[6] Take away the words, and we cannot think as well. Language is always changing, and new words appear every day. But old words disappear, too, and that can be very dangerous. L'Engle thinks that people need large vocabularies to express themselves well. We have dozens of words that have a similar meaning as the word "good," and all those choices allow people to select the word they prefer. Each word is a little different—"excellent" and "fine" do not mean quite the same thing—and that gives people more variety. If we all said "good" every time, everyone would sound the same. We would lose our individuality, and become identical and boring. As L'Engle showed in *A Wrinkle in Time*, conformity is not a good thing. It destroys the individual and drowns the soul. We need our own words so that we can express ourselves fully.

Inspirations

People always ask authors how they get their ideas. L'Engle gets hers by looking around her and seeing things that make her think. She read the word "tesseract" in a science article years ago and was fascinated by the concept. That fascination grew into a novel, and that novel was *A Wrinkle in Time*. She often has mental images of an idea, and then she wants to explore it. A few years ago, L'Engle read an article about heliopods. Heliopods are bits of flame that erupt from the sun, hit the end of outer space, and bounce back again. The idea fascinated her. She could see in her head these bits of sunlight bouncing off the end of the universe and that made her want to know more about them. She wants to ask questions and see if she can find some answers, and that means writing a story involving heliopods. She sends her characters to these places that intrigue her. They ask the questions for her.

But L'Engle doesn't have to find an answer to everything. She knows that some questions don't have answers. Others have answers she cannot understand. But the answers aren't all that matter. The questions themselves are important. She encourages her readers to always ask questions, particularly about important things. And she tells them not to let anyone stop them from asking. People have the right to be their own person and to ask their own questions. We may not get answers, but asking helps us think. We can learn things just by asking.

Advice for Writers

L'Engle has three suggestions for people who want to write:

> First, if you want to write, you need to keep an honest, unpublishable journal that nobody reads, nobody but you. Where you just put down what you think about life, what you think about things, what you think is fair and what you think is unfair. And second, you need to read. You can't be a writer if you're not a reader. It's the great writers who teach us how to write. The third thing is to write. Just write a little bit every day. Even if it's for only half an hour—write, write, write.[7]

The key to all three suggestions for writing, as with many things in L'Engle's life, is practice and patience. The more you read, and the more you write, the better you will get. Madeleine L'Engle has been practicing for more than eighty years and she's only gotten better.

Interview with Madeleine L'Engle

This interview is excerpted from an online interview at Amazon.com, conducted by Karin Snelson.

AMAZON.COM: Many of your novels are about children who are brilliant in perhaps nontraditional, unrecognizable ways, like Meg in *A Wrinkle in Time*. They strike a chord with many kids who feel misunderstood or shunned as geeks. Have you received much feedback like that from young readers?

MADELEINE L'ENGLE: Oh, there are a lot of Megs running around the country. Megs who are Meg's age and also Megs who have grown up who tell me they were Megs when they were Meg's age. I get over 100 letters a week, and not all of them are from kids—in fact, most of them are not. They are from ages 16 on up to 80. And there are a lot of nonconformists around, sort of coming out from under the covers.

AMAZON.COM: In *Meet the Austins* the children call conformists "muffins" and they celebrate "anti-muffins." And in *A Wrinkle in Time* the people of Camazotz are all happy because they're alike, free from individual responsibility, and free from pain. Rereading this as an adult made me think of the soma-happy characters in [Aldous Huxley's] *Brave New World* [1932]. How would you articulate the dangers of conformity in society?

MADELEINE L'ENGLE: Well, that's what the media wants. We'd buy more things, we'd think less, we wouldn't have any fun. If you have to conform you can't have fun. And I was never a good conformist; it didn't work well.

AMAZON.COM: Where does your strong grasp of the healthy family come from? I think that's one of the things I like the best about your books . . .

these strong, intimate families that are unparalleled in most people's experiences.

MADELEINE L'ENGLE: Well, I may have written about the best of us, but I was really writing about my own family. My husband was a wonderful father. When we were in our mid 60s he looked at me in horror and he said, "Darling! We never had time for a midlife crisis!" And we never had one! Life was too busy. But we do have wonderful children and wonderful grandchildren.

AMAZON.COM: In *A Wrinkle in Time*, Meg risks her life to save her physicist father from the dreaded It. And in *Meet the Austins*, Maggy redeems herself in the eyes of her new family only when she fights to defend her new brother, John. Your characters are capable of truly selfless acts. Why do you think kids need heroes?

MADELEINE L'ENGLE: Oh, life would be so dull without them! We wouldn't have anything to aim for, you know? What do you do without heroes? I always needed somebody that I wanted to be as good as, if not better than.

AMAZON.COM: Who are your heroes?

MADELEINE L'ENGLE: Oh, most of my heroes are long dead. George MacDonald was one. He was excommunicated from his church because he refused to believe that a god of love would wipe out two-thirds of the planet as being unworthy of his attention. And I think that's fine. I agree. In fiction, I loved *Emily of New Moon*. Lucy Maud Montgomery is better known for her Anne books, but I loved Emily. Emily wanted to be a writer; Emily saw the transcendence, so she was definitely a hero who allowed me to be different!

AMAZON.COM: I don't remember thinking of *A Wrinkle in Time* as being particularly religious when I first read it, but now I'm very aware of all the biblical references and the larger sense of evil that Meg and her cohorts are fighting. Would you say that your children's books have an overtly Christian message?

MADELEINE L'ENGLE: No. I would say they have an overtly "the universe is basically benign" message. I mean, that the maker is a benign maker. But I don't want to limit it to Christians. Years ago I was autographing in a college bookstore and a young man came up to me at the end and said, "I really like what you've been saying, but I haven't read your books because I hear they're religious." And all my little red flags of warning unfurled and flapped in the wind and I said, "What do you mean by religious? Khomeini is religious. Jerry Falwell is religious . . . what do you mean by religious?" And then I heard myself saying, "My religion is subject to change without notice!" And I thought that was my revelation for the year. If it's not, it's dead! So it's still open to change without notice.

AMAZON.COM: What messages would you like children to take away from your books?

MADELEINE L'ENGLE: Be brave! Have courage! Don't fear! Do what you think you ought to do, even if it's nontraditional. Be open. Be ready to change.

AMAZON.COM: I saw that you wrote the foreword to *Companion to Narnia* and wondered if people ever compare you to C. S. Lewis . . .

MADELEINE L'ENGLE: C. S. Lewis has more answers than I do. And I have more questions. It's a difference with people who were born before the First World War, which he was, and those born afterwards. I was born just afterwards. The First World War really broke the backbone of the century, and it did make a difference in what people thought. Those born before that war still can find war a tenable metaphor. I cannot. A friend of mine says, "There is no such thing as redemptive violence. Violence does not redeem." And I agree with that.

AMAZON.COM: Your books are rich with references to science and scientific exploration and ultra-intellectual characters, and yet occasionally you are deemed "anti-intellectual." Do you think that's because people are used to pitting science against religion?

MADELEINE L'ENGLE: Yes, and I have never seen any reason to do that. All science can do is open up a wider understanding of the universe. I mean, God doesn't change, we change in what we believe. And because we no longer think we're a little planet with everything whirling around us—the center of the universe—our idea of God has changed along with that . . . Everything big we discover in science changes what we think about God, unless we insist on keeping him in a white nightgown.

Timeline

1918 Madeleine L'Engle Camp is born in New York City on November 29.

1923 She writes her first story.

1930 The Camps move to Europe.

1932 They move back to the United States, and L'Engle attends Ashley Hall in Charleston, South Carolina.

1935 L'Engle's father dies.

1937 L'Engle enters Smith College in Northampton, Massachusetts.

1941 Madeleine graduates from Smith College with honors in English and moves to Greenwich Village in New York City to become a writer.

1943 L'Engle is cast in *The Cherry Orchard* during the summer and meets actor Hugh Franklin.

1944 She begins to write under the name Madeleine L'Engle.

1945 She writes her first novel, *The Small Rain*, and Vanguard Press publishes it.

1946 L'Engle and Franklin are married on January 26. They purchase Crosswicks, a farmhouse near Goshen, Connecticut.

1947 The Franklins' daughter, Josephine, is born in June.

1952 Franklin retires from the theater, and the family moves to Crosswicks, where they reside year-round. They buy a general store in Goshen. The Franklins' son, Bion, is born on March 24.

1957 The Franklins adopt seven-year-old Maria.

1959 L'Engle begins to write *A Wrinkle in Time*.

1960 The Franklins sell their store. They move back to New York City.

1962 Farrar, Straus & Giroux buys and publishes *A Wrinkle in Time*.

1963 *A Wrinkle in Time* wins the Newbery Medal.

1965 L'Engle becomes writer-in-residence at the Cathedral Church of St. John the Divine.

1981 Smith College awards the Smith Medal to L'Engle.

1986 Hugh Franklin dies.

1988 *Star*gazer*, a film about L'Engle, is narrated by Julie Harris, produced and directed by Martha Wheelock, and distributed by Ishtar Films.

1997 L'Engle receives a World Fantasy Award for lifetime achievement from the World Fantasy Convention.

1998 She receives the Margaret A. Edwards Award for lifetime achievement for writing in young adult fiction.

1999 Bion dies. L'Engle's first great-grandchild is born.

2004 On November 17, President George W. Bush awards the National Humanities Medal to L'Engle.

Selected Reviews from *School Library Journal*

Camilla
March 1982

Grade 7 and up—"I am Camilla Dickinson and no one else and no one else is me." The first-person narrator of this New York City story incidentally explores the nature of God, death, friendship, and self-awareness, all against the background of a plot exploring a range of the manifestations of love. Camilla discovers that the love her parents have for one another does not prevent her childish mother from seeking attention from another man. She sees her best friend's parents abuse love with quarreling and drink until they separate. She herself falls in love for the first time, with

Frank, her friend's brother. Camilla sees the complexity of human relationships: how different two people's expectations for the same situation may be, how intentions may produce unanticipated results, how external circumstance may present unwilled but unchangeable barriers. Frank's parents separate, Camilla's are reconciled, and Camilla loses Frank, who leaves town with his dad, before they have experienced even a first kiss. This is an ambitious book that explores a range of techniques (flashbacks when Camilla consents to being psychoanalyzed by her friend Luisa) and character (a young man who lost both legs in a war). Readers will sympathize with the protagonist as she learns that growing up has satisfactions, but that happiness is not necessarily always among them.

Many Waters
November 1986

Grade 6 and up—Fans of the Murry family will welcome this tangental [sic] return to the "Time Trilogy" books (Farrar) as L'Engle spins another uniquely metaphysical fantasy, this time using the twins, Sandy and Dennys, at age 15, as her protagonists. On a cold day, Dennys absent-mindedly requests his father's computer to take them "someplace warm."

Suddenly, it's the twins' turn to tessor [to travel by tesseract], and they end up in a desert so hot that they nearly die of sun poisoning. As they meet the small people who inhabit it, including Lemach, Shem, Ham, Japheth, and finally, Noah, they realize that they are in the world as it existed before the Great Flood. What follows is an entertaining description of life in this ancient time and place, when angels and fallen angels walked the earth, and small mammoths could call unicorns into existence. The story is more tension than plot: the tension of the Nephilim, fallen angels whose power on earth seems somehow threatened by the mysterious arrival of the twins; the sexual tension that both Sandy and Dennys feel as they are drawn to Yalith, Noah's youngest daughter; and the tension that readers feel, wondering how those protagonists not mentioned in Genesis (the twins and Yalith) are going to survive the Flood, which is plainly imminent throughout the book. This suspense lacks the urgency found in the other books of the trilogy, however, mainly because the characters are subservient to atmosphere, incident, and ideas. It is as hard for readers to tell the twins apart as it is for Noah. One is curious as to how they will escape, but hardly worried. The strength of this book lies in its haunting descriptions of a time resonant of our own. Its weakness is a pat ending and characters so slightly drawn that we hardly care.

Troubling a Star
October 1994

Grade 6 and up—In this fourth book about the Austin family, Vicky is almost 16. Adam Eddington, her budding love interest in *A Ring of Endless Light* (Dell, 1981), is headed for a marine-biology internship in Antarctica. His wealthy great-aunt is so taken with Vicky that she gives the young woman a trip there for her birthday. However, politics and international wheeling and dealing quickly turn the opportunity of a lifetime into a fight for survival as Vicky becomes a pawn in the struggles that surround her. Readers know that trouble is in store from the onset, as each chapter begins with an italicized paragraph of her terrified musings while she waits to be rescued from the iceberg upon which she is stranded. Most of the intrigue is centered on the tiny South American country of Vespugia, which will be familiar to readers of *A Swiftly Tilting Planet* (Farrar, 1978). There is no fantasy here, though—only human foibles such as greed and waste as the environmentalists who want to protect this continent and the various interest groups, who prefer to use it for personal gain, squabble. The narrative is interspersed with the poetry Vicky often uses to express her feelings, and with lively descriptions of the wildlife and habitats of Antarctica. The mystery itself is fairly transparent, even predictable. Those YAs who are accustomed to more contemporary realism in their novels may find the Austins, with their wholesome, intellectual lifestyle and their thoughtful, well-connected friends, as close to fantasy as one can get while remaining on Earth. Hopefully, though, they'll be able to suspend their disbelief long enough to enjoy Vicky's adventure.

List of
Selected Works

An Acceptable Time. New York, NY: Farrar,
    Straus & Giroux, 1989.
The Anti-Muffins. New York, NY: The Pilgrim
    Press, 1980.
The Arm of the Starfish. New York, NY: Farrar,
    Straus & Giroux, 1965.
And Both Were Young. New York, NY: Lothrop,
    Lee & Shepard Co., 1949.
Camilla Dickinson. New York, NY: Simon
    and Schuster, 1951; republished as
    Camilla, New York, NY: Delacorte
    Press, 1965.
Dance in the Desert. New York, NY: Farrar,
    Straus & Giroux, 1969.
Dragons in the Waters. New York, NY: Farrar,
    Straus & Giroux, 1976.

A Full House: An Austin Family Christmas. Wheaton, IL: Harold Shaw Publishers, 1999.

A House Like a Lotus. New York, NY: Farrar, Straus & Giroux, 1984.

Ladder of Angels: Scenes from the Bible Illustrated by Children of the World. New York, NY: Harper & Row, 1979.

Lines Scribbled on an Envelope and Other Poems. New York, NY: Farrar, Straus & Giroux, 1969.

Many Waters. New York, NY: Farrar, Straus & Giroux, 1986.

Meet the Austins. New York, NY: Vanguard Press, 1960.

The Moon by Night. New York, NY: Farrar, Straus & Giroux, 1963.

A Ring of Endless Light. New York, NY: Farrar, Straus & Giroux, 1980.

A Swiftly Tilting Planet. New York, NY: Farrar, Straus & Giroux, 1978.

Troubling a Star. New York, NY: Farrar, Straus & Giroux, 1994.

A Wind in the Door. New York, NY: Farrar, Straus & Giroux, 1973.

A Wrinkle in Time. New York, NY: Farrar, Straus & Giroux, 1962.

The Young Unicorns. New York, NY: Farrar, Straus & Giroux, 1968.

List of
Selected Awards

ALAN (Assembly on Literature for Adolescents) Award for Outstanding Contribution to Adolescent Literature from the National Council of Teachers of English (1986)

Margaret A. Edwards Award, in honor of an author's lifetime achievement for writing books that have been popular with teenagers (1998)

National Humanities Medal (2004)

New England Round Table of Children's Literature Honor Certificate (1974)

World Fantasy Lifetime Achievement Award (1997)

The Moon by Night (1963)
Austrian State Literary Prize (1969)

A Ring of Endless Light (1980)
California Young Reader Medal (1982)
Colorado Children's Book Award (1983)
Dorothy Canfield Fisher Children's Book
    Award (1981)
Newbery Honor Award (1981)
Newbery Honor Book (1980)

A Swiftly Tilting Planet (1978)
American Book Award (1980)
International Reading Association Children's
    Book Choice (IRA/CBC) Award (1979)

A Wrinkle in Time (1962)
Runner-up, Hans Christian Andersen Award (1964)
John Newbery Medal (1963)
Lewis Carroll Shelf Award (1965)
Sequoyah Award (1965)

Glossary

allegory The symbolism of objects, places, or people in a story. For example, a person represents anger and a place represents peace. A story can be an allegory if the entire story represents something else, such as the struggle between good and evil.

boarding school A school where the students are provided with meals and lodging.

chronos Chronos is the quantitative measure of time. It is ordinary time, real time, time that we can measure with our watches. Chronos is the type of time in which the Austin stories take place.

Episcopalian A member of the Protestant Episcopal Church representing the Anglican communion in the United States.

farandolae Microscopic organisms in our bodies.

genre A category of writing that is determined by setting, style, characters, and plot elements. Mystery is a genre. Fantasy is another genre.

journal A book of private notes and observations.

kairos An ancient Greek word meaning the "right or opportune moment." It is idealized or perfect time. It means time that cannot be measured. The Murrys and O'Keefes travel in the kairos type of time.

Lewis Carroll Shelf Award A major children's book award given out annually from 1958 to 1979. The winning books were considered to have the same quality as Carroll's *Alice in Wonderland.*

literary agent Someone who helps authors to sell their novels, stories, plays, or scripts to publishers or producers and negotiates with the publishers or producers to get the works into bookstores and libraries or performed on stage or in film.

manuscript The text of a book that an author sends to a publisher.

microbes Tiny organisms too small to see with the naked eye.

mitochondria Microscopic bodies found in the cells of almost all living organisms.

A mitochondrion contains enzymes responsible for the conversion of food to usable energy.

pigeonholed To be assigned a narrow space. An author can be pigeonholed if people believe that he or she can only write one type of book.

platonic A relationship that does not involve sex or romance.

protagonist The main character in a story.

Sequoyah Award This annual award is given by the state of Oklahoma to the book chosen by students across the state. The Sequoyah Book Award program is sponsored by the Oklahoma Library Association.

tesseract A cube cubed, or hypercube. A tesseract is a fourth-dimensional object.

World War I Often called "the Great War," this was the first war to involve nations from several different continents. It lasted from 1914 to 1918, and changed the fate of many nations.

For More Information

Due to the changing nature of Internet links, the Rosen Publishing Group, Inc., has developed an online list of Web sites related to the subject of this book. This site is updated regularly. Please use this link to access the list:

http://www.rosenlinks.com/lab/male

For Further Reading

Chase, Carole F. *Suncatcher: A Study of Madeleine L'Engle and Her Writing.* Philadelphia, PA: Innisfree Press, 1998.

Gonzalez, Doreen. *Madeleine L'Engle: Author of A Wrinkle in Time.* New York, NY: Dillon Press, 1991.

Jones, Raymond E. *A Literature Guide to A Wrinkle in Time* by Madeleine L'Engle. Cambridge, MA: Book Wise, Inc., 1991.

Shaw, Luci. *The Swiftly Tilting Worlds of Madeleine L'Engle* (Wheaton Literary Series). Wheaton, IL: Harold Shaw Publishers, 1998.

Wytenbroek, J. R. *Nothing Is Ordinary: The Extraordinary Vision of Madeleine L'Engle.* San Bernardino, CA: Borgo Press, 1996.

Bibliography

Chase, Carole F. *Madeleine L'Engle, Suncatcher: Spiritual Vision of a Storyteller*. Philadelphia, PA: Innisfree Press, 1997.

Chase, Carole F. *Suncatcher: A Study of Madeleine L'Engle and Her Writing*. Philadelphia, PA: Innisfree Press, 1998.

"Connecticut Women's Hall of Fame: Madeleine L'Engle." Retrieved August 1, 2004 (http://www.cwhf.org/hall/lengle/lengle.htm).

Currier, Tammy L. "Madeleine L'Engle." Retrieved August 4, 2004 (http://www.teenreads.com/authors/au-lengle-madeleine.asp).

Danielson, Julie. "Madeleine L'Engle." Retrieved July 11, 2004 (http://web.utk.edu/~jdaniels/lenglepage.html).

Friedland, Joyce, and Rikki Kessler. *A Wrinkle in Time by Madeleine L'Engle: Study Guide*. Roslyn Heights, NY: Learning Links, 1982.

Gonzalez, Doreen. *Madeleine L'Engle: Author of A Wrinkle in Time*. New York, NY: Dillon Press, 1991.

Henneberger, Melinda. "'I Dare You': Madeleine L'Engle on God, 'The Da Vinci Code' and Aging Well." *Newsweek Entertainment*, May 7, 2004. Retrieved July 24, 2004 (http://msnbc.msn.com/id/4926262).

Hettinga, Donald R. *Presenting Madeleine L'Engle*. Twayne's U.S. Authors. New York, NY: Twayne, 1993.

Hettinga, Donald R. "A Wrinkle in Faith: The Unique Spiritual Pilgrimage of Madeleine L'Engle." Retrieved July 17, 2004 (http://www.ctlibrary.com/bc/1998/mayjun/8b3034.html).

Horowitz, Shel. "Madeleine L'Engle: Faith During Adversity." Retrieved August 15, 2004 (http://www.frugalfun.com/l'engle.html).

Jones, Raymond E. *A Literature Guide to A Wrinkle in Time by Madeleine L'Engle*. Cambridge, MA: Book Wise, Inc., 1991.

Lavin, Brian, John McWilliams, Jessica Weare, and Eli Weiss. "A Wrinkle in Time." Retrieved August 19, 2004 (http://www.math.brown.edu/~banchoff/Yale/project12).

L'Engle, Madeleine. "Acceptance Speech Upon Receiving the Margaret Edwards Award." American Library Association Lifetime Achievement Award for Writing in the Field of Young Adult Literature, June 27, 1998. Retrieved November 9, 2004 (http://www.madeleinelengle.com/reference/libspeech.htm).

L'Engle, Madeleine. "Random House Author Spotlight: Madeleine L'Engle." Retrieved August 1, 2004 (http://www.randomhouse.com/kids/author/results_spotlight.pperl?authorid=16446).

"Literary Analysis of Madeleine L'Engle's Books." Retrieved August 1, 2004 (http://mle_project.tripod.com/litanalysis.htm).

"More Junior Authors: Madeleine L'Engle Autobiographical Sketch." Retrieved August 16, 2004 (http://www.wheaton.edu/learnres/ARCSC/collects/sc03/bio.htm).

"A New Wrinkle: A Conversation with Madeleine L'Engle." Retrieved July 11, 2004 (http://www.amazon.com/exec/obidos/ts/feature/6238/103-5220903-3682637).

"Notes on Madeleine L'Engle's Lecture, 'Story as Truth,' at Goshen College on Thursday September 12, 1996." Retrieved July 23, 2004 (http://www.geocities.com/Athens/Acropolis/8838/goshrec.html).

Pritzker, Karen. "Writer Hero: Madeleine L'Engle." Retrieved September 2, 2004 (http://myhero.com/myhero/hero.asp?hero=engle).

Random House Books. "A Wrinkle in Time Guide." Retrieved August 22, 2004 (http://www.randomhouse.com/catalog/display.pperl?0440998050&view=tg).

"Raven's Reviews: Madeleine L'Engle." Retrieved August 7, 2004 (http://tatooine.fortunecity.com/leguin/405/ko/madeleinel.html).

Risher, Dee Dee. "Listening to the Story: A Conversation with Madeleine L'Engle." *The Other Side Online*, March–April 1998, Vol. 34, No. 2. Retrieved August 4, 2004 (http://www.theotherside.org/archive/mar-apr98/lengle.html).

Scaperlanda, María Ruiz. "Madeleine L'Engle: An Epic in Time." Retrieved August 2, 2004 (http://www.americancatholic.org/Messenger/Jun2000/feature1.asp).

Shaw, Luci. *The Swiftly Tilting Worlds of Madeleine L'Engle*. Wheaton Literary Series. Wheaton, IL: Howard Shaw Publishers, 1998.

St. Yves, Suzanne. "Into the Depths of the Human Heart: Madeleine L'Engle's Search for God." Culture Watch. Retrieved August 4, 2004 (http://www.sojo.net/index.cfm?action=magazine.article&issue=soj9503&article=950331).

"Teaching the Madeleine L'Engle Tetralogy: Using Allegory and Fantasy as Antidote to Violence." Retrieved August 20, 2004 (http://www3.wcu.edu/~mwarner/LEnglepaper.html).

"The Time Quartet by Madeleine L'Engle." Retrieved August 16, 2004 (http://www.kidsreads.com/series/series-time-author.asp).

Weatherstone, Lunaea. "Madeleine L'Engle." Retrieved July 23, 2004 (http://www.lunaea.com/words/lengle/fiction.html).

Wong, Christina. "Paradigms, Prayer, and Particle Physics: An Interview with Madeleine L'Engle." *Music, Movies and Mayhem Magazine*, No. 15, January 15, 1997. Retrieved July 13, 2004 (http://www.gopherp.com/gopprd1cissue15.htm#lengle).

Wytenbroek, J. R. *Nothing Is Ordinary: The Extraordinary Vision of Madeleine L'Engle*. San Bernardino, CA: Borgo Press, 1996.

Zarin, Cynthia. "The Storyteller. Fact, Fiction, and the Books of Madeleine L'Engle." *New Yorker*, April 12, 2004, pp. 60–67.

Source Notes

Introduction

1. Madeleine L'Engle, *A Circle of Quiet* (San Francisco, CA: HarperSanFrancisco, 1972), p. 198.
2. Madeleine L'Engle, *A Wrinkle in Time* (New York, NY: Farrar, Straus & Giroux, 1962), p. 31.

Chapter 1

1. Madeleine L'Engle, *The Summer of the Great-Grandmother* (New York, NY: Farrar, Straus & Giroux, 1974), p. 1.
2. Madeleine L'Engle, "Random House Author Spotlight: Madeleine L'Engle." Retrieved August 1, 2004 (http://www.randomhouse.com/kids/author/results_spotlight.pperl?authorid=16446).
3. Madeleine L'Engle, "A New Wrinkle: A Conversation with Madeleine L'Engle."

Retrieved July 11, 2004 (http://www.amazon.com/exec/obidos/ts/feature/6238/103-5220903-3692637).

4. Ibid.
5. Ibid.
6. Madeleine L'Engle, *A Wrinkle in Time* (New York, NY: Farrar, Straus & Giroux, 1962), p. 123.

Chapter 2

1. Madeleine L'Engle, "Random House Author Spotlight: Madeleine L'Engle." Retrieved August 1, 2004 (http://www.randomhouse.com/kids/author/results_spotlight.pperl?authorid=16446).
2. Madeleine L'Engle, "A New Wrinkle: A Conversation with Madeleine L'Engle." Retrieved July 11, 2004 (http://www.amazon.com/exec/obidos/ts/feature/6238/103-5220903-3692637).
3. Madeleine L'Engle, *Two-Part Invention: The Story of a Marriage* (New York, NY: Farrar, Straus & Giroux, 1988), p. 10.
4. Ibid., p. 47.

Chapter 3

1. Shel Horowitz, "Madeleine L'Engle: Faith During Adversity." Retrieved August 15, 2004 (http://www.frugalfun.com/l'engle.html). Originally published in *Global Art Review*, 1991.
2. María Ruiz Scaperlanda, "Madeleine L'Engle: An Epic in Time." *Messenger*, June 2000. Retrieved August 2, 2004 (http://www.americancatholic.org/Messenger/Jun2000/feature1.asp).

3. Karen Pritzker, "Writer Hero: Madeleine L'Engle." Retrieved September 2, 2004 (http://myhero.com/myhero/hero.asp?hero=engle).
4. Ibid.
5. Horowitz.
6. Madeleine L'Engle, "A New Wrinkle: A Conversation with Madeleine L'Engle." Retrieved July 11, 2004 (http://www.amazon.com/exec/obidos/ts/feature/6238/103-5220903-3692637).

Chapter 4

1. Shel Horowitz, "Madeleine L'Engle: Faith During Adversity." Retrieved August 15, 2004 (http://www.frugalfun.com/l'engle.html). Originally published in *Global Art Review*, 1991.
2. Ibid.
3. Madeleine L'Engle, "Acceptance Speech Upon Receiving The Margaret Edwards Award." American Library Association Lifetime Achievement Award for Writing in the Field of Young Adult Literature. June 27, 1998. Retrieved November 9, 2004 (http://www.madeleinelengle.com/reference/libspeech.htm).
4. Ibid.

Chapter 5

1. Madeleine L'Engle, "Random House Author Spotlight: Madeleine L'Engle." Retrieved August 1, 2004 (http://www.randomhouse.com/kids/author/results_spotlight. pperl?authorid=16446).

2. Madeleine L'Engle, *The Other Side of the Sun* (New York, NY: Ballantine, 1990), p. 220.

3. Dee Dee Risher, "Listening to the Story: A Conversation with Madeleine L'Engle." *The Other Side Online*, March–April 1998, Vol. 34, No. 2. Retrieved August 4, 2004 (http://www.theotherside. org/archive/mar-apr98/lengle.html).

4. Melinda Henneberger, "'I Dare You': Madeleine L'Engle on God, 'The Da Vinci Code' and Aging Well." *Newsweek Entertainment*. May 7, 2004. Retrieved July 24, 2004 (http://msnbc.msn.com/ id/4926262).

5. Madeleine L'Engle, "Acceptance Speech Upon Receiving the Margaret Edwards Award." American Library Association Lifetime Achievement Award for Writing in the Field of Young Adult Literature. June 27, 1998. Retrieved November 9, 2004 (http://www.madeleine/engle.com/reference/ libspeech.htm).

6. Madeleine L'Engle, *A Circle of Quiet* (San Francisco, CA: HarperSanFrancisco, 1972), p. 124.

7. Henneberger.

Chapter 6

1. María Ruiz Scaperlanda, "Madeleine L'Engle: An Epic in Time." *Messenger*, June 2000. Retrieved August 2, 2004 (http://www.americancatholic.org/ Messenger/Jun2000/feature1.asp).

2. Madeleine L'Engle, "Acceptance Speech Upon Receiving The Margaret Edwards Award." American Library Association Lifetime Achievement Award for Writing in the Field of Young Adult Literature. June 27, 1998. Retrieved November 9, 2004 (http://www.madeleine/engle.com/reference/libspeech.htm).

3. Madeleine L'Engle, *Penguins and Golden Calves* (New York, NY: Shaw Books, 2003), p. 133.

4. Madeleine L'Engle, "Acceptance Speech Upon Receiving The Margaret Edwards Award." June 27, 1998.

5. Shel Horowitz, "Madeleine L'Engle: Faith During Adversity." Retrieved August 15, 2004 (http://www.frugalfun.com/l'engle.html). Originally published in *Global Art Review*, 1991.

6. Madeleine L'Engle, *The Small Rain* (New York, NY: Vanguard Press, 1945), p. 122.

7. Madeleine L'Engle, "Random House Author Spotlight: Madeleine L'Engle." Retrieved August 1, 2004 (http://www.randomhouse.com/kids/author/results_spotlight.pperl?authorid=16446).

Index

About the Author

Aaron Rosenberg was ten years old when he first discovered Madeleine L'Engle's *A Wrinkle in Time*. He soon read the rest of the Murry saga. Those books and the works of Andre Norton and Ursula K. LeGuin hooked him on fantasy novels and inspired him to pursue a career in writing. He earned a B.A. degree in English and Creative Writing, and an M.A. degree in English Literature. He writes educational books and novels, and has published short stories and novellas in magazines and anthologies. He also writes books for the Star Trek: Starfleet Corps of Engineers series. In 2005, he finished his first fantasy novel. He lives in New York City.

Photo Credits

Cover © Judith Petrovich, p. 2 © Kenneth S. Lewis

Designer: Tahara Anderson;
Editor: Kathy Kuhtz Campbell;
Photo Researcher: Hillary Arnold